Sizzling
MEXICAN
RECIPES

PUBLICATIONS INTERNATIONAL, LTD.

Microwave ovens vary in wattage. The cooking times given in this publication are approximate. Use the cooking times as guidelines and check for doneness before adding more time. Consult manufacturer's instructions for suitable microwave-safe cooking dishes.

Sizzling MEXICAN RECIPES

Salsas & Snacks

Deluxe Fajita Nachos

2½ cups shredded, cooked
    chicken
1 package (1.27 ounces)
    LAWRY'S® Spices &
    Seasonings for Fajitas
⅓ cup water
8 ounces tortilla chips
1¼ cups (5 ounces) shredded
    Cheddar cheese

1 cup (4 ounces) shredded
    Monterey Jack cheese
1 large tomato, chopped
1 can (2¼ ounces) sliced
    ripe olives, drained
¼ cup sliced green onions
    Salsa

In medium skillet, combine chicken, Spices & Seasonings for
Fajitas and water; blend well. Bring to a boil; reduce heat and
simmer 3 minutes. In large shallow ovenproof platter, arrange
chips. Top with chicken and cheeses. Place under broiler to melt
cheese. Top with tomato, olives, green onions and desired amount
of salsa. *Makes 4 appetizer servings*

PRESENTATION: *Serve with guacamole and sour cream.*

SUBSTITUTION: *1¼ pounds cooked ground beef can be used in
place of shredded chicken.*

HINT: *For a spicier version, add sliced jalapeños.*

Spicy Empanadas

1 can (8¾ ounces)
    garbanzo beans,
    drained
1 teaspoon vegetable oil
¼ cup minced fresh onion
2 tablespoons minced
    green bell pepper
¼ teaspoon LAWRY'S®
    Garlic Powder with
    Parsley
2 tablespoons currants
2 tablespoons chopped
    pitted ripe olives

1 package (1.25 ounces)
    LAWRY'S® Taco Spices
    & Seasonings
1 teaspoon lemon juice
¼ cup (1 ounce) shredded
    Monterey Jack cheese
    All-purpose flour
1 sheet frozen puff pastry,
    thawed
1 egg yolk, beaten

Preheat oven to 400°F. In food processor or blender, place garbanzo beans. Pulse 30 seconds to chop finely; set aside. In large skillet, heat oil. Add onion, bell pepper and Garlic Powder with Parsley; sauté 3 to 4 minutes or until vegetables are crisp-tender. Add beans, currants, olives, Taco Spices & Seasonings and lemon juice; cook until mixture thickens, stirring occasionally. Remove from heat; stir in cheese.

On lightly floured surface, roll out pastry sheet to approximately 18×10-inch rectangle; cut out six to eight 4-inch circles. Spoon equal amounts of filling onto half of each circle; fold pastry over to form half circle. Press edges together with fork to seal. Place empanadas on greased baking sheet; brush with egg yolk. Bake 18 to 20 minutes or until golden brown. Garnish as desired.

Makes 6 to 8 empanadas

PRESENTATION: *Great with salsa, dairy sour cream and peeled avocado slices.*

HINT: *Double recipe for more appetizers.*

Festive Chicken Dip

1½ pounds boneless skinless chicken breasts, finely chopped (about 3 cups)
¼ cup lime juice, divided
2 garlic cloves, minced
1 teaspoon salt
½ teaspoon ground black pepper
1 can (16 ounces) refried beans
1½ cups sour cream, divided
1 package (1¼ ounces) dry taco seasoning mix, divided
1 tablespoon picante sauce

1 avocado, chopped
1 tablespoon olive oil
1 cup (4 ounces) shredded sharp Cheddar cheese
1 small onion, finely chopped
2 tomatoes, finely chopped
1 can (2¼ ounces) sliced black olives, drained and chopped
1 bag (10 ounces) tortilla chips
Fresh cilantro for garnish

Place chicken in small bowl. Sprinkle with 3 tablespoons lime juice, garlic, salt and pepper; mix well. Set aside.

Combine beans, ½ cup sour cream, 2½ tablespoons taco seasoning and picante sauce in medium bowl. Spread bean mixture in bottom of shallow 2-quart casserole dish.

Combine avocado and remaining 1 tablespoon lime juice in small bowl; sprinkle over bean mixture. Combine remaining 1 cup sour cream and 2½ tablespoons taco seasoning in small bowl; set aside.

Heat oil in large skillet over high heat until hot; add chicken in single layer. Do not stir. Cook about 2 minutes or until chicken is brown on bottom. Turn chicken and cook until other side is brown and no liquid remains. Break chicken into separate pieces with fork. Layer chicken, sour cream mixture, cheese, onion and tomatoes over avocado mixture. Top with olives. Refrigerate until completely chilled. Serve with chips. Garnish with cilantro.

Makes 8 cups dip

Favorite recipe from **National Broiler Council**

Festive Chicken Dip

Rio Grande Quesadillas

2 cups shredded, cooked
chicken
1 package (1.25 ounces)
LAWRY'S® Taco Spices
& Seasonings
¾ cup water
1 can (16 ounces) refried
beans
6 large flour tortillas

1½ cups (6 ounces) shredded
Monterey Jack cheese
¼ cup chopped pimiento
¼ cup chopped green
onions
¼ cup chopped fresh
cilantro
Vegetable oil

In medium skillet, combine chicken, Taco Spices & Seasonings
and water. Bring to a boil; reduce heat and simmer, uncovered,
15 minutes. Stir in refried beans. On half of each tortilla, spread
approximately ⅓ cup of chicken-bean mixture. Layer ⅙ each of
cheese, pimiento, green onions and cilantro on top. Fold each
tortilla in half. In large skillet, heat a small amount of oil and
quickly fry folded tortilla on each side until slightly crisp. Repeat
with each folded tortilla.   *Makes 6 servings*

PRESENTATION: *Cut each quesadilla in quarters and serve with
chunky salsa and guacamole.*

No Way, José Lentil Salsa

2 fresh medium tomatoes
2 cups cooked USA Lentils
1 can (4 ounces) diced
green chilies
1 cup finely chopped onion
2 tablespoons chopped
fresh cilantro *or*
2 teaspoons ground
coriander

1 tablespoon red wine
vinegar
1 tablespoon fresh lime
juice
2 cloves minced garlic
½ teaspoon salt

Chop tomatoes and place in large bowl. Add remaining
ingredients and mix well. Chill before serving.

Makes 4 servings

Favorite recipe from **USA Dry Pea & Lentil Council**

Rio Grande Quesadillas

South-of-the-Border Vegetable Kabobs

5 cloves garlic, peeled
½ cup A.1.® BOLD Steak
    Sauce
¼ cup margarine, melted
1 tablespoon finely
    chopped fresh cilantro
¾ teaspoon ground cumin
¼ teaspoon coarsely
    ground black pepper
⅛ teaspoon ground red
    pepper

3 ears corn, cut crosswise
    into 1½-inch-thick
    slices and blanched
3 medium plum tomatoes,
    cut into ½-inch slices
1 small zucchini, cut
    lengthwise into thin
    slices
1 cup baby carrots,
    blanched

Mince 1 garlic clove; halve remaining garlic cloves and set aside. In small bowl, combine steak sauce, margarine, cilantro, minced garlic, cumin and peppers; set aside.

Alternately thread vegetables and halved garlic cloves onto 6 (10-inch) metal skewers. Grill kabobs over medium heat for 7 to 9 minutes or until done, turning and basting often with steak sauce mixture. Remove from skewers; serve immediately.

Makes 6 servings

Quick Corn Bread with Chilies 'n' Cheese

1 package (12 to 16 ounces)
    corn bread or corn
    muffin mix
1 cup (4 ounces) shredded
    Monterey Jack cheese,
    divided

1 can (4 ounces) chopped
    green chilies, drained
1 envelope LIPTON®
    Recipe Secrets®
    Vegetable Soup Mix

Prepare corn bread mix according to package directions; stir in ½ cup cheese, chilies and vegetable soup mix. Pour batter into lightly greased 8-inch baking pan; bake as directed. While warm, top with remaining ½ cup cheese. Cool completely on wire rack. To serve, cut into squares.

Makes 16 servings

South-of-the-Border Vegetable Kabobs

El Dorado Rice Casserole

1 can (14½ ounces) whole
    peeled tomatoes, cut up
1½ cups chicken broth
1 medium onion, chopped
1 tablespoon vegetable oil
1 cup uncooked long-grain
    rice

1 teaspoon LAWRY'S®
    Garlic Salt
1 cup dairy sour cream
1 can (4 ounces) diced
    green chilies, drained
1½ cups (6 ounces) shredded
    Monterey Jack cheese

Drain tomatoes, reserving juice. Add reserved juice to broth to
make 2½ cups liquid; set aside. In medium saucepan, sauté onion
in oil until tender. Add tomato-broth mixture, tomatoes, rice and
Garlic Salt. Bring to a boil. Reduce heat; cover and simmer 25
minutes or until liquid is absorbed. In small bowl, combine sour
cream and chilies. In 1½-quart casserole, layer ½ of prepared rice,
½ of sour cream mixture and ½ of cheese. Repeat. Bake at 350°F
20 minutes or until bubbly.
Makes 6 servings

PRESENTATION: *Top casserole with avocado and pimiento slices.*

Black Bean Turkey Pepper Salad

¾ pound fully cooked
    honey-roasted turkey
    breast, cut into ¼-inch
    cubes
1 small red bell pepper, cut
    into ¼-inch cubes
1 small yellow bell pepper,
    cut into ¼-inch cubes
1 can (15 ounces) black
    beans, rinsed and
    drained

1 cup thinly sliced green
    onions
¾ cup chopped fresh
    cilantro
2 tablespoons olive oil
1 tablespoon red wine
    vinegar
1 teaspoon ground cumin
¼ teaspoon cayenne pepper

1. In large bowl combine turkey, red and yellow peppers, black
beans, onions and cilantro.

2. In small bowl whisk together oil, vinegar, cumin and cayenne
pepper. Fold dressing into turkey mixture. Cover and refrigerate
1 hour.
Makes 6 servings

Favorite recipe from **National Turkey Federation**

El Dorado Rice Casserole

South-of-the-Border Salad

2 cups smoked fish, fresh or frozen
½ medium head lettuce, torn into 2-inch pieces
1 large peeled avocado, cut into 1-inch pieces
1 medium tomato, chopped
1 cup diagonally sliced celery
1 cup (4 ounces) shredded mild Cheddar cheese
½ cup cooked, drained garbanzo beans
½ cup chopped green onions
½ cup grated carrot
½ cup buttermilk-style salad dressing
1 package (4 ounces) tortilla chips, lightly crushed

Thaw fish if frozen. Break fish into bite-sized pieces. Combine all ingredients except salad dressing and tortilla chips. Toss well. Add dressing and tortilla chips and serve immediately.

Makes 6 servings

Favorite recipe from **Florida Department of Agriculture and Consumer Services, Bureau of Seafood and Aquaculture**

Santa Fe Potato Salad

5 medium white potatoes
½ cup vegetable oil
¼ cup red wine vinegar
1 package (1.25 ounces) LAWRY'S® Taco Spices & Seasonings
1 can (7 ounces) whole kernel corn, drained
⅔ cup sliced celery
⅔ cup shredded carrots
⅔ cup chopped red or green bell pepper
2 cans (2¼ ounces each) sliced ripe olives, drained
½ cup chopped red onion
2 tomatoes, wedged and halved

In large saucepan, cook potatoes in boiling water to cover until tender, about 40 minutes; drain. Cool slightly; cut into cubes. In small bowl, combine oil, vinegar and Taco Spices & Seasonings. Add to warm potatoes and toss gently to coat. Cover; refrigerate at least 1 hour. Gently fold in remaining ingredients. Refrigerate until thoroughly chilled.

Makes 10 servings

PRESENTATION: *Serve in lettuce-lined bowl with hamburgers or deli sandwiches.*

South-of-the-Border Salad

Hot Taco Salad

¾ **pound lean ground beef**
    (80% lean)
½ **cup chopped onion**
1 **package (6.8 ounces)**
    RICE-A-RONI® Beef
    Flavor
½ **cup salsa**
1 **teaspoon chili powder**

4 **cups shredded lettuce**
1 **medium tomato, chopped**
½ **cup (2 ounces) shredded**
    Monterey Jack or
    Cheddar cheese
½ **cup crushed tortilla**
    chips (optional)

1. In large skillet, brown ground beef and onion; drain. Remove from skillet; set aside.

2. In same skillet, prepare Rice-A-Roni Mix as package directs.

3. Stir in meat mixture, salsa and chili powder; continue cooking over low heat 3 to 4 minutes or until heated through.

4. Arrange lettuce on serving platter. Top with rice mixture, tomato and cheese. Top with tortilla chips, if desired.

Makes 5 servings

Mexican Pork Salad

1 **pound boneless pork**
    loin, cut into
    3×½×¼-inch strips
4 **cups shredded lettuce**
1 **medium orange, peeled,**
    sliced and quartered
1 **medium avocado, peeled,**
    seeded and diced

1 **small red onion, sliced**
    and separated into
    rings
1 **tablespoon vegetable oil**
1 **teaspoon chili powder**
¾ **teaspoon salt**
½ **teaspoon dried oregano**
    leaves, crushed
¼ **teaspoon ground cumin**

Place lettuce on serving platter. Arrange orange, avocado and red onion over lettuce. Heat oil in large skillet; add chili powder, salt, oregano and cumin. Add pork loin strips and stir-fry over medium-high heat 5 to 7 minutes or until pork is tender. Spoon hot pork strips over lettuce mixture. Serve immediately.

Makes 4 servings

Favorite recipe from **National Pork Producers Council**

Hot Taco Salad

Soups, Stews & Chilies

Santa Fe Taco Stew

1 tablespoon vegetable oil
½ cup diced onion
½ teaspoon LAWRY'S®
  Garlic Powder with
  Parsley
1 package (1.25 ounces)
  LAWRY'S® Taco Spices
  & Seasonings
1 can (28 ounces) diced
  tomatoes, undrained
1 can (15 ounces) pinto
  beans, drained
1 can (8¾ ounces) whole
  kernel corn, drained

1 can (4 ounces) diced
  green chilies, drained
1 cup beef broth
½ teaspoon cornstarch
1 pound pork butt or beef
  chuck, cooked and
  shredded
Dairy sour cream
  (garnish)
Tortilla chips (garnish)
Fresh cilantro (garnish)

In Dutch oven or large saucepan, heat oil. Add onion and Garlic Powder with Parsley; sauté 2 to 3 minutes until onion is translucent and tender. Add Taco Spices & Seasonings, tomatoes, beans, corn and chilies; blend well. In small bowl, gradually blend broth into cornstarch using wire whisk. Stir into stew. Stir in cooked meat. Bring to a boil, stirring frequently. Reduce heat to low; simmer, uncovered, 30 minutes, stirring occasionally. (Or, simmer longer for a thicker stew.) *Makes 8 servings*

PRESENTATION: *Garnish each serving with sour cream, tortilla chips and fresh cilantro, if desired.*

VARIATION: *Substitute 3 cups cooked, shredded chicken for pork or beef.*

Santa Fe Taco Stew

Creamy Gazpacho

1 cup undiluted
  CARNATION®
  Evaporated Skimmed
  Milk
1¾ cups (14.5-ounce can)
  CONTADINA® Recipe
  Ready Diced Tomatoes
2 cups tomato juice
3 tablespoons lemon juice
2 tablespoons olive oil
1 clove garlic, minced
½ teaspoon salt
¼ teaspoon ground black
  pepper

¼ teaspoon hot pepper
  sauce
2 cups (2 medium) peeled,
  seeded and diced
  cucumbers
½ cup diced green bell
  pepper
½ cup diced onion
  Garnishes: Plain low fat
  or nonfat yogurt, diced
  cucumber, bell pepper
  and onion (optional)

Place evaporated skimmed milk, tomatoes, tomato juice, lemon juice, olive oil, garlic, salt, pepper and hot pepper sauce in blender; cover and blend thoroughly. (Blender container will be very full.)

Pour into serving bowl or tureen and add cucumbers, bell pepper and onion; stir thoroughly. Chill. Serve cold; garnish as desired.

Makes about 7 (1-cup) servings

South-of-the-Border Chicken Soup

3 tablespoons vegetable oil
3 corn tortillas cut into
  ½-inch strips
⅓ cup chopped onion
⅔ cup chopped green and
  red peppers
1 clove garlic, minced
¼ cup all-purpose flour

2 (12-ounce) cans chicken
  broth
1 teaspoon chili powder
2 cups cubed cooked
  chicken
1 (16-ounce) can VEG-ALL®
  Mixed Vegetables, with
  liquid

Heat oil in skillet; add tortilla strips and fry, stirring constantly, until golden. Drain on paper towel-lined plate. Add onion and peppers; cook until soft. Add garlic and stir in flour; gradually stir in chicken broth. Add remaining ingredients and heat through. Top with tortilla strips.

Makes 4 to 6 servings

Creamy Gazpacho

Tex-Mex Chicken & Rice Chili

1 package (6.8 ounces)
RICE-A-RONI® Spanish
Rice
2¾ cups water
2 cups chopped cooked
chicken or turkey
1 can (15 or 16 ounces)
kidney beans or pinto
beans, rinsed and
drained
1 can (14½ or 16 ounces)
tomatoes or stewed
tomatoes, undrained

1 medium green bell
pepper, cut into ½-inch
pieces
1½ teaspoons chili powder
1 teaspoon ground cumin
½ cup (2 ounces) shredded
Cheddar or Monterey
Jack cheese (optional)
Sour cream (optional)
Chopped cilantro
(optional)

1. In 3-quart saucepan, combine rice-vermicelli mix, contents of
seasoning packet, water, chicken, beans, tomatoes, green pepper,
chili powder and cumin. Bring to a boil over high heat.

2. Reduce heat to low; simmer, uncovered, about 20 minutes or
until rice is tender, stirring occasionally.

3. Top with cheese, sour cream and cilantro, if desired.

Makes 4 servings

Salsa Corn Soup with Chicken

3 quarts chicken broth
2 pounds boneless skinless
chicken breasts,
cooked and diced
2 (10-ounce) packages
frozen corn kernels,
thawed

4 (11-ounce) jars
NEWMAN'S OWN® All
Natural Salsa
4 large carrots, cooked and
diced

Bring chicken broth to a boil in Dutch oven. Add chicken, corn,
salsa and carrots. Bring to a boil. Reduce heat and simmer until
carrots are tender.

Makes 8 servings

Tex-Mex Chicken & Rice Chili

Nacho Cheese Soup

1 package (about 5 ounces)
  dry au gratin potatoes
1 can (about 15 ounces)
  whole kernel corn,
  undrained
2 cups water
1 cup salsa
2 cups milk

1½ cups (6 ounces)
  SARGENTO® Classic
  Supreme® Shredded
  Cheese For Tacos
1 can (about 2 ounces)
  sliced ripe olives,
  drained
Tortilla chips (optional)

In large saucepan, combine potatoes, dry au gratin sauce mix, corn with liquid, water and salsa. Heat to a boil; reduce heat. Cover and simmer 25 minutes or until potatoes are tender, stirring occasionally. Add milk, taco cheese and olives. Cook until cheese is melted and soup is heated through, stirring occasionally. Garnish with tortilla chips. *Makes 6 servings*

Chili Blanco

½ pound diced turkey
  breast (optional)
1 tablespoon vegetable oil
½ cup diced celery
½ cup fresh or canned
  Anaheim chilies
½ cup chopped onion
2 cups water
1 can (16 to 19 ounces)
  small white or red
  kidney beans, drained
1 cup diced fresh tomatoes

1 cup diced zucchini
½ teaspoon salt
½ teaspoon ground cumin
⅛ teaspoon black pepper
⅛ teaspoon ground
  cayenne pepper
Condiments: Shredded
  low fat cheese,
  chopped onion,
  chopped cilantro and
  diced tomatoes
Corn or flour tortillas

Brown turkey in oil in medium saucepan; drain. Add celery, chilies and onion; cook until tender. Add remaining ingredients except condiments and tortillas; mix well. Bring to a boil; reduce heat and simmer 30 minutes. Serve with condiments and tortillas. *Makes 4 servings*

Favorite recipe from **California Table Grape Commission**

Nacho Cheese Soup

30-Minute Chili Olé

1 cup chopped onion
2 cloves garlic, minced
1 tablespoon vegetable oil
2 pounds ground beef
1 (15-ounce) can tomato
 sauce
1 (14½-ounce) can stewed
 tomatoes
¾ cup A.1.® Steak Sauce
1 tablespoon chili powder

1 teaspoon ground cumin
1 (16-ounce) can black
 beans, rinsed and
 drained
1 (11-ounce) can corn,
 drained
Shredded cheese, sour
 cream and chopped
 tomato for garnish

In 6-quart heavy pot, over medium-high heat, sauté onion and garlic in oil until tender. Add beef; cook and stir until browned. Drain; stir in tomato sauce, stewed tomatoes, steak sauce, chili powder and cumin. Heat to a boil; reduce heat to low. Cover; simmer for 10 minutes, stirring occasionally. Stir in beans and corn; simmer, uncovered, for 10 minutes. Serve hot; garnish with cheese, sour cream and tomato.

Makes 8 servings

Baja Corn Chowder

¼ cup butter or margarine
3 cans (17 ounces each)
 whole kernel corn,
 drained, divided
1 medium red bell pepper,
 diced
2 cups chicken broth
1 quart half-and-half
1 can (7 ounces) diced
 green chilies, drained

1 package (1.27 ounces)
 LAWRY'S® Spices &
 Seasonings for Fajitas
2 cups (8 ounces) shredded
 Monterey Jack cheese
½ teaspoon LAWRY'S®
 Seasoned Pepper
Hot pepper sauce to taste

In Dutch oven or large saucepan, melt butter. Add one can of corn and bell pepper; sauté 5 minutes. Remove from heat. In food processor or blender, place remaining two cans of corn and chicken broth; process until smooth. Add to Dutch oven with half-and-half, chilies and Spices & Seasonings for Fajitas. Return to heat. Bring just to a boil, stirring constantly. Remove from heat; blend in cheese, Seasoned Pepper and hot pepper sauce.

Makes 4 to 6 servings

Albóndigas Soup

1 pound ground beef
¼ cup long-grain rice
1 egg
1 tablespoon chopped
    fresh cilantro
1 teaspoon LAWRY'S®
    Seasoned Salt
¼ cup ice water
2 cans (14½ ounces each)
    chicken broth

1 can (14½ ounces) whole
    peeled tomatoes,
    undrained and cut up
¼ cup chopped onion
1 rib celery, diced
1 large carrot, diced
1 medium potato, diced
¼ teaspoon LAWRY'S®
    Garlic Powder with
    Parsley

In medium bowl, combine ground beef, rice, egg, cilantro, Seasoned Salt and ice water; form into small meatballs. In large saucepan, combine broth with vegetables and Garlic Powder with Parsley. Bring to a boil; add meatballs. Reduce heat; cover and simmer 30 to 40 minutes, stirring occasionally.

Makes 6 to 8 servings

PRESENTATION: *Serve with lemon wedges and warm tortillas.*

HINT: *For a lower salt version, use homemade chicken broth or low sodium chicken broth.*

Avocado Orange Soup

2 large ripe avocados,
    pitted
1 cup fresh orange juice
1 cup plain yogurt

½ teaspoon TABASCO®
    pepper sauce
¼ teaspoon salt
Orange slices

In food processor or blender, blend avocados and orange juice. Add yogurt, TABASCO sauce and salt. Blend until smooth. Refrigerate until ready to serve. Garnish with orange slices.

Makes 4 servings

StarKist® Vegetable Gazpacho

1 large onion, quartered
1 medium zucchini, halved lengthwise
1 yellow or crookneck squash, halved lengthwise
1 red bell pepper
1 yellow bell pepper
¾ cup bottled olive oil vinaigrette dressing
1 can (6 ounces) STARKIST® Solid White Tuna, drained and chunked

3 pounds firm ripe tomatoes, chopped
2 cucumbers, peeled, seeded and chopped
2 to 3 cloves fresh garlic, minced or pressed
½ cup fresh sourdough bread crumbs
1½ to 2 cups tomato juice

Preheat broiler. Brush onion quarters, zucchini halves, squash halves and whole peppers with dressing; reserve remaining dressing. Broil 6 to 8 minutes, turning occasionally, until vegetables are roasted and pepper skins blister and turn black. Remove from broiler. Place peppers in paper bag; close bag and let stand 15 minutes before peeling. Cool remaining vegetables. Peel skin from peppers; seed and remove membranes.

Cut roasted vegetables into large pieces; place in food processor bowl. Process until coarsely chopped. Transfer to large bowl; add tuna, tomatoes, cucumbers, garlic, bread crumbs, 1½ cups tomato juice and remaining dressing. Blend thoroughly. Add remaining ½ cup tomato juice to thin, if necessary.   *Makes 6 to 8 servings*

PREP TIME: *30 minutes*

Tacos, Enchiladas & More

Skillet Steak Fajitas

½ cup **A.1.**® **Steak Sauce**
½ cup **mild, medium or hot thick and chunky salsa**
1 **(1-pound) beef flank or bottom round steak, thinly sliced**
1 **medium onion, thinly sliced**
1 **medium green bell pepper, cut into strips**
1 **tablespoon margarine**
8 **(6½-inch) flour tortillas, warmed**

Blend steak sauce and salsa. Place steak in glass dish; coat with ¼ cup salsa mixture. Cover; chill 1 hour, stirring occasionally.

In large skillet, over medium-high heat, cook onion and pepper in margarine for 3 minutes or until tender. Remove with slotted spoon; set aside. In same skillet, cook and stir steak for 5 minutes or until done. Add remaining salsa mixture, onion and pepper; cook until heated through. Serve with tortillas and your favorite fajita toppings, if desired.

Makes 4 servings

Border Scramble

1 pound BOB EVANS
    FARMS® Original
    Recipe Roll Sausage
1½ cups chopped cooked
    potatoes
1½ cups chopped onions
1½ cups chopped tomatoes
¾ cup chopped green bell
    pepper
¼ to ½ cup picante sauce

½ to 1 tablespoon hot
    pepper sauce
½ teaspoon garlic powder
½ teaspoon salt
4 (9-inch) flour tortillas
2 cups prepared meatless
    chili
½ cup (2 ounces) shredded
    Cheddar cheese

Crumble sausage into large skillet. Cook over medium heat until browned, stirring occasionally. Drain off any drippings. Add remaining ingredients except tortillas, chili and cheese; simmer 20 minutes. To warm tortillas, place between paper towels; microwave 1 minute at HIGH. Place 1 cup sausage mixture in center of each tortilla; fold tortilla over filling. Heat chili in small saucepan until hot, stirring occasionally. Top each folded tortilla with ½ cup chili and 2 tablespoons cheese. *Makes 4 servings*

Chicken Feta Fajitas

1 tablespoon lime juice
1 teaspoon chili powder
1 teaspoon ground cumin
3 boneless skinless chicken
    breast halves (about
    1 pound), cut into
    strips
2 tablespoons vegetable oil
1 onion, sliced

1 red pepper, cut into
    strips
1 package (8 ounces)
    ATHENOS® Feta
    Natural Cheese,
    crumbled
6 flour tortillas (8 inches),
    warmed

• Mix juice, chili powder and cumin in medium bowl. Add chicken; toss lightly.

• Heat oil in large skillet over medium heat. Add chicken mixture; cook and stir 3 minutes. Add onion and pepper; continue cooking 3 minutes or until chicken is cooked through.

• Stir in cheese. Spoon chicken mixture onto tortillas; fold in half.

Makes 6 servings

Border Scramble

Tuna Fiesta Soft Tacos

⅓ cup mayonnaise
½ teaspoon garlic salt
½ teaspoon lemon pepper
   seasoning
1 can (6 ounces)
   STARKIST® Solid
   White or Chunk Light
   Tuna, drained and
   flaked
¼ cup chopped celery
1 hard-cooked egg,
   chopped
2 tablespoons finely
   chopped green onion

2 tablespoons finely
   chopped green bell
   pepper
1 tablespoon drained
   chopped pimiento
6 flour tortillas (6 inches
   each), warmed
1 cup shredded iceberg
   lettuce
½ cup shredded Colby or
   Monterey Jack cheese
Salsa (optional)

In large bowl, combine mayonnaise, garlic salt, lemon pepper seasoning, tuna, celery, egg, onion, bell pepper and pimiento; mix thoroughly. Place generous ¼ cup filling on one side of each tortilla; top with lettuce and cheese. Fold tortilla over; serve with salsa, if desired. *Makes 6 servings*

Breakfast Quesadillas

1 pound BOB EVANS
   FARMS® Original
   Recipe Roll Sausage
4 eggs
4 (10-inch) flour tortillas

2 cups (8 ounces) shredded
   Monterey Jack cheese
½ cup chopped green
   onions with tops
½ cup chopped tomato
Sour cream and salsa

Crumble sausage into large skillet. Cook over medium heat until sausage is browned, stirring occasionally. Drain off any drippings. Remove sausage to paper towels; set aside. Add eggs to same skillet; scramble until eggs are set but not dry. Remove eggs; set aside. Place 1 tortilla in same skillet. Top with half of each eggs, cheese, sausage, onions and tomato. Heat until cheese melts; top with another tortilla. Remove from skillet; cut into six equal wedges. Repeat with remaining tortillas, eggs, cheese, sausage, onions and tomato to make second quesadilla. Serve hot with sour cream and salsa. Refrigerate leftovers. *Makes 4 servings*

Tuna Fiesta Soft Taco

Huevos Rancheros Tostados

1 can (8 ounces) tomato
    sauce
⅓ cup prepared salsa or
    picante sauce
¼ cup chopped fresh
    cilantro *or* thinly sliced
    green onions
4 large eggs

Butter or margarine
4 corn tortillas (6 inches),
    crisply fried *or* 4
    prepared tostada shells
1 cup (4 ounces)
    SARGENTO® Classic
    Supreme® Shredded
    Cheese For Tacos

Combine tomato sauce, salsa and cilantro; heat in microwave oven or in saucepan over medium-high heat until hot. Fry eggs in butter, sunny side up. Place one egg on each tortilla; top with sauce. Sprinkle with taco cheese. *Makes 4 servings*

VARIATION: *Spread tortillas with heated refried beans before topping with eggs, if desired.*

Tacos

1 pound BOB EVANS
    FARMS® Original
    Recipe or Zesty Hot
    Roll Sausage
1 (8-ounce) jar taco sauce
1 package taco shells (10 to
    12 count)
2 cups (8 ounces) shredded
    Cheddar cheese

1 large onion, chopped
2 tomatoes, chopped
¼ head iceberg lettuce,
    shredded
    Fresh cilantro sprigs and
    bell pepper triangles
    (optional)

Preheat oven to 350°F. Crumble sausage into medium skillet; cook over medium-high heat until browned, stirring occasionally. Drain off any drippings. Stir in taco sauce. Bring to a boil. Reduce heat to low; simmer 5 minutes. Meanwhile, bake taco shells until warm and crisp. To assemble tacos, place 2 tablespoons sausage mixture in each taco shell and top evenly with cheese, onion, tomatoes and lettuce. Garnish with cilantro and pepper triangles, if desired. Serve hot. Refrigerate any leftover filling. *Makes 10 to 12 servings*

Huevos Rancheros Tostado

Bean and Vegetable Burritos

1 tablespoon olive oil
1 medium onion, thinly
    sliced
1 jalapeño pepper, seeded,
    minced
1 tablespoon chili powder
3 cloves garlic, minced
2 teaspoons dried oregano
    leaves, crushed
1 teaspoon ground cumin
1 large sweet potato,
    baked, cooled, peeled,
    diced *or* 1 can
    (16 ounces) yams in
    syrup, drained, rinsed,
    diced

1 can black beans or pinto
    beans, drained, rinsed
1 cup frozen whole kernel
    corn, thawed, drained
1 green bell pepper,
    chopped
2 tablespoons lime juice
¾ cup (3 ounces) shredded
    reduced fat Monterey
    Jack cheese
4 (10-inch) flour tortillas
    Low fat sour cream
    (optional)

Preheat oven to 350°F. Heat oil in large saucepan or Dutch oven over medium-high heat. Add onion and cook, stirring often, 10 minutes or until golden. Add jalapeño, chili powder, garlic, oregano and cumin; stir 1 minute. Add 1 tablespoon water and stir; remove from heat. Stir in sweet potato, beans, corn, green pepper and lime juice.

Spoon 2 tablespoons cheese in center of each tortilla. Top with 1 cup filling. Fold all 4 sides around filling to enclose. Place burritos seam side down on baking sheet. Cover with foil and bake 30 minutes or until heated through. Serve with sour cream, if desired.
Makes 4 servings

Bean and Vegetable Burrito

Rice & Bean Burritos

FILLING

1 tablespoon olive or
  vegetable oil
½ cup sliced green onions
1 jalapeño pepper, seeded
  and chopped
2 to 3 cloves garlic, minced
½ pound lean ground beef,
  turkey or chicken

2 cups water
1 can (14½ ounces)
  chopped tomatoes,
  undrained
1 package (8 ounces)
  FARMHOUSE®
  Mexican Beans & Rice
Salt and pepper

BURRITO FIXINGS

6 large *or* 12 small flour
  tortillas, softened
Shredded Cheddar
  cheese

Sour cream
Prepared salsa

For filling, in large skillet, heat oil until hot. Cook and stir onions, jalapeño and garlic in hot oil until garlic is tender but not brown. Add ground meat; cook until meat is no longer pink. Add water and undrained tomatoes; bring to a boil. Add beans & rice and contents of seasoning packet. Reduce heat; cover and simmer 25 minutes. Season to taste with salt and pepper.

To assemble burritos, place ⅔ cup meat mixture in center of large tortilla (⅓ cup for small tortillas). Top with shredded cheese, sour cream and salsa. Fold up burrito style and serve immediately.

Makes 6 servings

Red Chili Tortilla Torte

2 cans (16 ounces) pinto
  beans or black beans,
  rinsed and drained
¼ cup low-salt chicken
  broth
1 tablespoon vegetable oil
2 large onions, sliced
2 red bell peppers, cut into
  ¼-inch strips
2 zucchini, thinly sliced

2 cloves garlic, minced
1 cup whole kernel corn
1 teaspoon ground cumin
½ teaspoon salt
¼ teaspoon cayenne pepper
6 (8-inch) flour tortillas
2 cups NEWMAN'S OWN®
  All Natural Salsa
2 cups (8 ounces) shredded
  Monterey Jack cheese

In food processor, combine pinto beans and chicken broth. Process until smooth; set aside. Heat oil in large nonstick skillet over medium heat. Add onions, bell peppers, zucchini and garlic; sauté until softened, 10 to 12 minutes. Add corn, cumin, salt and cayenne pepper; cook about 2 minutes.

Heat oven to 375°F. Grease 8-inch round baking dish. Spread ½ cup of pinto bean mixture on one flour tortilla; place on bottom of baking dish. Spoon 1 cup of the onion mixture on top of the beans. Spoon ⅓ cup of Newman's Own® All Natural Salsa on top of onion mixture; top with ⅓ cup of cheese. Repeat with remaining ingredients, ending with cheese. Bake until heated through, about 45 minutes. Let stand 10 minutes; cut into wedges to serve. *Makes 8 to 10 servings*

Spicy Burrito Burgers

6 tablespoons prepared mild salsa, divided	**1 pound ground beef**
1 can (4 ounces) diced green chilies, divided	**4 (6-inch) flour tortillas**
¼ cup sour cream	**1 cup shredded lettuce**
Dash hot pepper sauce	**½ cup (2 ounces) shredded Cheddar cheese with taco seasonings**

Combine 2 tablespoons salsa, 2 tablespoons chilies, sour cream and hot pepper sauce in small bowl; set aside.

Combine beef, remaining 4 tablespoons salsa and remaining chilies in large bowl; mix well. Shape into four 4-inch oval patties.

Grill burgers over medium coals 8 to 10 minutes for medium or until desired doneness is reached, turning halfway through grilling time.

Place 1 burger in center of 1 tortilla. Top with one-quarter of the lettuce, cheese and sour cream mixture. Bring edges of tortilla together over top of burger; secure with toothpick if necessary. Remove toothpick before serving. *Makes 4 servings*

Tex-Mex Chicken Fajitas

6 boneless skinless chicken
breast halves (about
1½ pounds), cut into
strips
½ cup LAWRY'S® Mesquite
Marinade with Lime
Juice*
3 tablespoons plus
1½ teaspoons vegetable
oil, divided
1 small onion, sliced and
separated into rings
1 medium-sized green bell
pepper, cut into strips

¾ teaspoon LAWRY'S®
Garlic Powder with
Parsley
½ teaspoon hot pepper
sauce
1 medium tomato, cut into
wedges
2 tablespoons chopped
fresh cilantro
Flour tortillas, warmed
1 medium lime, cut into
wedges

Pierce chicken several times with fork; place in large resealable
plastic bag or bowl. Pour Mesquite Marinade with Lime Juice
over chicken; seal bag or cover bowl. Refrigerate at least 30
minutes. Heat 1 tablespoon plus 1½ teaspoons oil in large skillet.
Add onion, bell pepper, Garlic Powder with Parsley and hot
pepper sauce; sauté 5 to 7 minutes or until onion is crisp-tender.
Remove vegetable mixture from skillet; set aside. Heat remaining
2 tablespoons oil in same skillet. Add chicken; sauté 8 to 10
minutes or until chicken is no longer pink in center, stirring
frequently. Return vegetable mixture to skillet with tomato and
cilantro; heat through.   *Makes 4 to 6 servings*

PRESENTATION: *Serve with flour tortillas and lime wedges. Top
with dairy sour cream, guacamole, salsa and pitted ripe olives as
desired.*

*One package (1.27 ounces) Lawry's® Spices & Seasonings for
Fajitas, ¼ cup lime juice and ¼ cup vegetable oil can be
substituted.

Tacos Picadillos

¾ **pound ground pork**
1 **medium onion, chopped**
½ **teaspoon ground**
    cinnamon
½ **teaspoon ground cumin**
1 **can (14½ ounces)**
    DEL MONTE® Mexican
    Recipe Stewed
    Tomatoes

⅓ **cup DEL MONTE®**
    Seedless Raisins
⅓ **cup toasted chopped**
    almonds
6 **flour tortillas**

In large skillet, brown meat with onion and spices over medium-high heat. Season to taste with salt and pepper, if desired. Stir in tomatoes and raisins. Cover and cook 10 minutes. Remove cover; cook over medium-high heat 5 minutes or until thickened, stirring occasionally. Just before serving, stir in almonds. Fill tortillas with meat mixture; roll to enclose. Garnish with lettuce, cilantro and sour cream, if desired. Serve immediately.

Makes 6 servings

HELPFUL HINT: *If ground pork is not available, boneless pork may be purchased and ground in food processor. Cut pork into 1-inch cubes before processing.*

Fantastic Pork Fajitas

1 **pound pork strips**
2 **teaspoons vegetable oil**
½ **medium onion, peeled**
    and sliced

1 **green pepper, seeded and**
    sliced
4 **flour tortillas, warmed**

Heat large nonstick skillet over medium-high heat. Add oil; heat until hot. Add pork strips, onion and pepper slices to skillet and stir-fry quickly 4 to 5 minutes. Roll up portions of the meat mixture in flour tortillas and serve with purchased salsa, if desired.

Makes 4 servings

Favorite recipe from **National Pork Producers Council**

Ensenada Fish Tacos

10 ounces halibut or orange
    roughy fillets, cut into
    1-inch cubes
1 tablespoon vegetable oil
1 tablespoon lime juice
1 package (1.27 ounces)
    LAWRY'S® Spices &
    Seasonings for Fajitas
6 corn or flour tortillas
    (about 8 inches)
2½ cups shredded lettuce
½ cup diced tomatoes

¾ cup (3 ounces) shredded
    Monterey Jack or
    Cheddar cheese
2 tablespoons thinly sliced
    green onion
Dairy sour cream
    (garnish)
Guacamole (garnish)
Salsa (garnish)
Chopped fresh cilantro
    (garnish)

In shallow glass baking dish, place fish. Pour oil and lime juice over fish. Sprinkle with Spices & Seasonings for Fajitas; toss lightly to coat. Cover. Refrigerate 2 hours to marinate, occasionally spooning marinade over fish. In same dish, bake fish in 450°F oven 10 minutes or until fish flakes easily with fork; drain. To serve, evenly divide fish; place in center of each tortilla. Top with lettuce, tomatoes, cheese and green onion. Garnish as desired.
Makes 6 servings

Turkey Tacos

1 pound ground turkey
2 tablespoons minced
    dried onion
1 tablespoon chili powder
1 teaspoon paprika
½ teaspoon *each* cumin,
    dried oregano and salt
¼ teaspoon garlic powder

⅛ teaspoon black pepper
10 taco shells
1 to 2 tomatoes, chopped
2 to 3 cups shredded
    lettuce
⅔ cup shredded reduced-
    fat Cheddar cheese

In large nonstick skillet over medium-high heat, cook and stir turkey, onion and seasonings 5 to 6 minutes or until turkey is no longer pink. Spoon mixture evenly into taco shells and top with tomatoes, lettuce and cheese.
Makes 5 servings

Favorite recipe from **National Turkey Federation**

Ensenada Fish Tacos

Mexican Main Dishes

Classic Arroz con Pollo

2 tablespoons olive oil
1 broiler-fryer chicken
  (about 2 pounds),
  cut up
2 cups uncooked long-
  grain rice
1 cup chopped onion
1 medium-size red bell
  pepper, chopped
1 medium-size green bell
  pepper, chopped
1 clove garlic, minced
1½ teaspoons salt, divided

1½ teaspoons dried basil
4 cups chicken broth
1 tablespoon lime juice
⅛ teaspoon ground saffron
  or ½ teaspoon ground
  turmeric
1 bay leaf
2 cups chopped tomatoes
½ teaspoon ground black
  pepper
1 cup fresh or frozen green
  peas
Fresh basil for garnish

Heat oil in Dutch oven over medium-high heat until hot. Add chicken; cook 10 minutes or until browned, turning occasionally. Remove chicken; keep warm. Add rice, onion, red pepper, green pepper, garlic, ¾ teaspoon salt and basil to Dutch oven; cook and stir 5 minutes or until vegetables are tender and rice is browned. Add broth, lime juice, saffron and bay leaf. Bring to a boil; stir in tomatoes. Arrange chicken on top and sprinkle with remaining ¾ teaspoon salt and black pepper. Cover; reduce heat to low. Cook 20 minutes more. Stir in peas; cover and cook 10 minutes more or until fork can be inserted into chicken with ease and juices run clear, not pink. Remove bay leaf. Garnish with basil. Serve immediately.   *Makes 8 servings*

Favorite recipe from **USA Rice Council**

Classic Arroz con Pollo

Mexicali Beef & Rice

1 package (6.8 ounces)
  RICE-A-RONI® Beef
  Flavor
1 cup frozen corn *or* 1 can
  (8 ounces) whole
  kernel corn, drained
½ cup chopped red or
  green bell pepper

1 pound lean ground beef
  (80% lean)
Salt and pepper
  (optional)
Salsa (optional)
Sour cream (optional)

1. Prepare Rice-A-Roni Mix as package directs, stirring in frozen corn and red pepper during last 10 minutes of cooking.

2. While Rice-A-Roni is simmering, shape beef into four ½-inch-thick patties.

3. In lightly greased second large skillet, cook beef patties over medium heat, about 4 minutes on each side or until desired doneness. Season with salt and pepper, if desired.

4. Serve rice topped with cooked beef patties, salsa and sour cream, if desired.   *Makes 4 servings*

Pork Tenderloin Mole

1½ pounds pork tenderloin
  (about 2 whole)
1 teaspoon vegetable oil
½ cup chopped onion
1 clove garlic, minced
1 cup Mexican-style chili
  beans, undrained
¼ cup chili sauce

¼ cup raisins
2 tablespoons water
1 tablespoon peanut butter
1 teaspoon unsweetened
  cocoa
Dash *each* salt, ground
  cinnamon and ground
  cloves

Place tenderloin in shallow baking pan. Roast at 350°F for 30 minutes or until juicy and slightly pink in center.

Heat oil in medium saucepan. Cook onion and garlic over low heat for 5 minutes. Combine onion and garlic with remaining ingredients in food processor; mix until almost smooth. Heat mixture in saucepan thoroughly over low temperature, stirring frequently. Serve over tenderloin slices.   *Makes 6 servings*

Favorite recipe from **National Pork Producers Council**

Mexicali Beef & Rice

Spicy Tuna Empanadas

1 can (6 ounces)
STARKIST® Solid White
or Chunk Light Tuna,
drained and flaked
1 can (4 ounces) diced
green chilies, drained
1 can (2¼ ounces) sliced
ripe olives, drained
½ cup shredded sharp
Cheddar cheese
1 chopped hard-cooked
egg

Salt and pepper to taste
¼ teaspoon hot pepper
sauce
¼ cup medium thick and
chunky salsa
2 packages (15 ounces
each) refrigerated pie
crusts
Additional salsa

In medium bowl, place tuna, chilies, olives, cheese, egg, salt, pepper and hot pepper sauce; toss lightly with fork. Add ¼ cup salsa and toss again; set aside. Following directions on package, unfold crusts (roll out slightly with rolling pin if you prefer thinner crust); cut 4 circles, 4 inches *each,* out of each crust. Place 8 circles on foil-covered baking sheets; wet edge of each circle with water. Top each circle with ¼ cup lightly packed tuna mixture. Top with remaining circles, stretching pastry slightly to fit; press edges together and crimp with fork. Cut slits in top crust to vent. Bake in 425°F oven 15 to 18 minutes or until golden brown. Cool slightly. Serve with additional salsa. *Makes 8 servings*

Spicy Tuna Empanadas